PUFFIN

What would y...
Wobble-de...

Colin West is one of Britain's fo........nse poets, and this collection finds him in fine comic form. Meet the unlikely mermaid, sympathize with the unsuccessful knitter, and eavesdrop at the ventriloquists' convention!

Hilarious poems of the absurd combine with verse that is slightly more whimsical and thought-provoking, and the poet's own quirky line drawings bring his world to life. *What would you do with a Wobble-dee-woo?* will have you grinning from ear to ear.

Born in London in 1951, Colin West attended both Wolverhampton College of Art and the Royal College of Art, where his tutor was Quentin Blake, who remains one of his favourite illustrators. He thinks many people today take themselves too seriously, and derives much of his own inspiration from the past. (He loves to collect old books, old photographs and photographic paraphernalia such as magic lantern slides). He has written and illustrated many children's books, this being his first volume of verse in Puffin.

What would you do with a WOBBLE·DEE·WOO?

Poems & Pictures by Colin West

PUFFIN BOOKS

PUFFIN BOOKS

Published by the Penguin Group
Penguin Books Ltd, 27 Wrights Lane, London W8 5TZ, England
Viking Penguin, a division of Penguin Books USA Inc.
375 Hudson Street, New York, New York 10014, USA
Penguin Books Australia Ltd, Ringwood, Victoria, Australia
Penguin Books Canada Ltd, 2801 John Street, Markham, Ontario, Canada L3R 1B4
Penguin Books (NZ) Ltd, 182–190 Wairau Road, Auckland 10, New Zealand

Penguin Books Ltd, Registered Offices: Harmondsworth, Middlesex, England

First published by Hutchinson Children's Books 1988
Published in Puffin Books 1991
10 9 8 7 6 5 4 3 2 1

Printed in England by Clays Ltd, St Ives plc
Set in Monophoto Bembo

CONTENTS

Introduction	9
The Unlikely Mermaid	10
Knock, Knock	12
Passers-by	13
Z	14
Park Regulations	15
Miss Murgatroyd	16
Mrs Jones	17
Leaflets	18
Good Homes for Kittens	19
Me and Amanda	20
Knitting	21
Things to collect	22
This House	23
Adelaide	24
Mr Lott's Allotment	24
Veronica	25
The Retired Sergeant Major	26
Who?	28
The New Boy	29
Our Playground	30
The Staff Room	31
The Bridle and the Saddle	32
Old Song Revisited	33
A Scarecrow Remembers	34
Insides	36
Nowhere-in-Particular	36
Worries and What to do with Them	37

The Three Salesmen 38
Whatnot 39
Let Basil go to Basildon 40
My Uncle's Umbrella 42
Rolling down a Hill 43
Sir Percy's Problem 44
Barge Pole 48
Juggler Jim 49
Borderline Case 50
The Trough 52
The Echo 53
Have You Ever? 54
Establishment 56
Uncle Paul 57
Archibald's Progress 58
Ben 60
Winter Term 61
Gordon Glass 62
Plodders 63
A Blackpool Ballad 64
Trampoline 66
Certificates 67
Four Tongue Twisters 68
The Missing Eskimo 70
Yo-yo 72
Joe 73
Wobble-dee-woo 74
School Day 75
Commuter 76
Me 76
The Cat and the King 77
Frank's Chair 78
Pogo Stick 79
Mr Burton 80
Moggy 82

My Dog   82
Sabre-toothed Tigers   83
The Wildebeest   84
Octopus   85
Lost Gloves   86
Pullover   87
Dressing Gown   87
I'll be in the Wardrobe, Wilma   88
Peter   89
Maybe to an Elephant   90
The Ventriloquists' Convention   91
Rosemary's Friends   92
Yesterday, Today and Tomorrow   93
Our Coconut Mat   94
Dining with Duke Humphrey   95
Poems, Poems, Everywhere   96

Introduction

Here are rhymes to read to others:
Fathers, mothers, sisters, brothers;
Here are poems in their dozens
For your grannies and your cousins;
Here are tales of crazy creatures
To be read to friends and teachers;
Here are songs and here are shanties
For your uncles and your aunties;
And in this book upon your shelf
Are words to keep just for yourself.

The Unlikely Mermaid

Please pardon my asking you, Irene,
But why do you sit on the stair,
As seaward you gaze out the window
As though there were somebody there?

   The ocean is calling me
   For to return,
   For I was a mermaid
   Before you were born.

Please pardon my ignorance, Irene,
I must seem remarkably dim.
I don't understand – *you* a mermaid?
I know for a fact you can't swim.

A mermaid does other things
Other than float,
Like singing a shanty
By clearing her throat.

Please pardon my doubting you, Irene,
I cannot believe what you say.
Your skin hasn't scales and your body
Resembles a fish in no way.

I wouldn't expect you to
Think it is true;
For I'm not a fire-breathing
Dragon like you.

Knock, Knock

No, I do not wish to hear
Another knock knock joke.
I've heard your knock knock
Jokes before,
So please don't knock knock
On my door.
I'll sure knock knock
Your block off
If you knock knock
Any more.

12

Passers-by

A passer-by
Was passing by
A by-pass,
And passing by
The by-pass
A passer-by
Passed by:
By passing by
A by-pass
As a passer-by
Passed by,
A passer-by
Was passed by
By a by-pass
Passer-by.

Z

I know a place called Zagazig.
I can't live there, it's much too big.

I know a place called Zyradow.
I lived there once, I don't know how.

I know a place called Zanzibar.
I can't go there, it's much too far.

I know a place called Zonguldak.
I went there once – I won't go back.

I know a place called Zhitomir.
I can't think why I'm staying here.

I know a place called Zug. I thought
I'd go there as a last resort . . .

Park Regulations

The rules upon this board displayed
Are here by all to be obeyed:

Keep off the grass. Don't scale the wall.
Don't throw, or kick, or bat a ball.
Don't pluck the flowers from their bed.
Don't feed the ducks with crusts of bread.
Bicycles may not be ridden.
Rollerskating is forbidden.
Dogs must be kept upon their leashes
And kept from chasing other species.
Dispose of litter thoughtfully.
Do not attempt to climb a tree
Or carve initials on the bark.
Don't play a wireless in the park
(Or any sort of instrument).
Don't build a fire or pitch a tent
And don't throw stones or gather sticks.
The gates are closed at half past six.

Observe these rules and regulations
(Signed) Head of Parks and Recreations.

Miss Murgatroyd

Together down the street they go,
Beneath the one umbrella,
Miss Murgatroyd and Montague,
The brute she calls her fella.

Miss Murgatroyd loves Montague,
Wrapped in his lanky arms,
She finds within his funny face
Lie all life's hidden charms.

She finds his charming countenance
Much sweeter than most men's is.
(Perhaps she needs a pair of specs,
Or else some contact lenses.)

Together down the street they go,
And so they will until a
Spoilsport tells Miss Murgatroyd
That . . . Monty's a gorilla.

Mrs Jones

Upon her old velocipede
Comes shaky Mrs Jones,
But is that dreadful rattling
Her bicycle – or bones?

Leaflets

Leaflets, leaflets, I like leaflets,
I love leaflets when they're free.
When I see a pile of leaflets,
I take one, or two (or three).

Banks are always good for leaflets –
They've got lots of leaflets there –
Leaflets on investing money:
How to be a Millionaire. ⊕ *na na*

And I go to my Gas Show Room,
For their leaflets are such fun,
And I visit travel agents –
They've got leaflets by the ton.

Leaflets, leaflets, I like leaflets,
I love leaflets when they're free.
When I see a pile of leaflets,
Something strange comes over me.

Theatre foyers offer leaflets:
What to see and how to book.
Stations, libraries and so on –
All have leaflets if you look.

I've got leaflets by the dozen,
I've got leaflets by the score,
I've got leaflets by the hundred,
Yet I always yearn for more.

Good Homes for Kittens

Who'd like a Siamese?
Yes, please.

An Angora?
I'd adora.

A Tabby?
Ma'be.

A Black and White?
All right.

A Tortoiseshell?
Oh, very well.

A Manx?
No thanx!

Me and Amanda

Me
    and
        Amanda
         meander,
      like
    rivers
  that
run
  to
    the
      sea.
        We
    wander
  at
    random,
       we're
         always
           in
          tandem:
           meandering
          Mandy
       and
        me.

Knitting

She tried to knit a nightcap,
She tried to knit a scarf,
She tried to knit a cardigan,
Too big, they were, by half.

She tried to knit a waistcoat,
She tried to knit a shawl,
She tried to knit a bobble hat:
They all turned out too small.

And now she's knitting knickers,
And if *they* do not fit,
We'll make her wear them anyhow
Until she's learned to knit . . .

Things to collect

What sort of things do you collect?
Postcards, stamps or badges,
Photographs or foreign coins,
Pens or pencil sharpeners?

Autographs or magazines,
Bottle tops or boxes,
Records, rings or handkerchiefs,
Ornaments or pictures?

Pebbles, shells or bits or bark,
Flowers, leaves or fossils,
Seaweed, driftwood, feathers, twigs?
What sort of things do *you* collect?

This House

This house, now you're away,
Misses you more each day;
Its every little room
Has its own special gloom.
The handles on the doors
Wait for a touch that's yours;
The sofa and the chairs
Long for your seat on theirs.
This house with just me in it
Misses you more each minute.

Adelaide

Adelaide is up a ladder.
Adelaide's an adder-upper.
She's an addled adder-upper,
Adding adders up a ladder.

Mr Lott's Allotment

Mr Lott's allotment
Meant a lot to Mr Lott.
Now Mr Lott is missed a lot
On Mr Lott's allotment.

Veronica

Adventurous Veronica
Upon her yacht *Japonica*
Is sailing to Dominica.
She blows her old harmonica
Each night beneath the spinnaker,
And dreams of seeing Monica,
Her sister, in Dominica.

The Retired Sergeant Major

His final round has long been fired,
And Sgt-Major Green (retired)
Within his garden may be found
For this is now his stamping ground.

He's up each day at crack of dawn
To give a haircut to his lawn,
And then, at 0600 hours,
He's off inspecting troops of flowers.

They hold their heads erect as if
Their very stems are frightened stiff,
And woe betide should one be bent,
Disgracing the whole regiment.

At noon, ex-Sgt-Major Green
In vegetable plot is seen,
Where in a bucket he will shove
Potatoes, for the peeling of.

Observe him stride about the place,
(No weed dare ever show its face)
And all the time he's on parade
He bears a highly-polished spade,

Until we see at eventide
Him armed with an insecticide,
For as the sun sinks in the west,
He wages war on Garden Pest.

Who?

Who's always there come rain or shine,
From eight o'clock till ten past nine?
Who's back again at half past three
As we are going home for tea?
Who wears a coat that's long and white,
And cap with badge that's big and bright?
Who's always cheerful, always nice?
Whose banner bears a strange device?
Who teaches us the Highway Code,
And sees us safely 'cross the road?
Who is it makes the traffic stop?
O Lady of the Lollipop!

The New Boy

Please, sir, I'm the new boy,
My trousers are corduroy,
My cap's the wrong colour,
My name is James Fuller.

I'm no good at games, sir,
But can tell you the names, sir,
Of all of our kings, sir,
From Norman to Windsor.

I have a pet hamster,
My mother's from Amster-
Dam, but my father's
As English as Arthur's.

I've brought a packed lunch, sir,
An apple to munch, sir,
Ham rolls and a number
Of cheese and cucumber.

I sang in the choir, sir,
When my voice was higher, sir,
But now that I've spoken,
You'll notice it's broken.

Please, sir, I'm the new boy,
My trousers are corduroy,
My cap's the wrong colour,
My name is James Fuller . . .

Our Playground

Our playground wouldn't be so bad
If it didn't slope so much
But as it is, when we play football,
We have to have two sides:
The Uphills and the Downhills;
And the Uphills always lose.

Life must be as sloping as our playground;
For there always seems to be two sides,
The Uphills and the Downhills;
And the Uphills always lose.

The Staff Room

The Staff Room is a mystery
Whose door is always shut.
It's not the sort of place for me,
It's where the teachers like to be
In rather close proximity.
They must enjoy it, but
To me it is a mystery
Whose door is always shut.

The Bridle and the Saddle

The bridle and the saddle
Fitted, I sit in the middle
Of the horse, but why I straddle
Such a creature is a riddle.

O, he's big and I am little.
And he no doubt thinks I'm idle,
And he knows my bones be brittle
As I hang on to the bridle.

But it doesn't seem to addle
Him that I am in a muddle
As I cower in the saddle
When we pass over each puddle.

Old Song Revisited

It was a feline fiddler
Who played a merry tune
Inspired a bovine acrobat
To leap over the moon;
A canine witness was amused
At shows of such buffoon-
Ery; a piece of crockery
Eloped with what? A spoon!

A Scarecrow Remembers

Head of straw and heart of wood,
With arms outstretched like this I've stood
For half a year in Hertfordshire.
My feet stuck in the mud.

Things could be worse, for I remember
One day early in November,
The children came from far and wide
Wheeling a barrow with another
Ragged fellow flopped inside.
But no sooner had I glimpsed my brother
Than they took him from his carriage
To a hilltop where they perched him on a pyre,
And they laughed to watch him perish
As they set his clothes on fire.

The sky that night was filled with light,
With shooting stars and rockets,
I stood my ground and made no sound
When sparks fell in my pockets.

Amidst the Bedlam I could see
Old Owl a-tremble in his tree,
And when the noise at last died down
The children all returned to town,
And left the bonfire smouldering,
And my poor brother mouldering
Till only ash remained.

Insides

I'm very grateful to my skin
For keeping all my insides in –
I do so hate to think about
What I would look like inside-out.

Nowhere-in-Particular

O, Nowhere-in-Particular
Is just the place for me,
I go there every now and then
For two weeks or for three.

And Doing Nothing Special there
Is what I like to do,
At Nowhere-in-Particular
For three weeks or for two.

Worries and What to do with Them

O, gather all your worries,
And put them in a box,
Then toss the box into the sea,
And you'll forget them presently.

Meanwhile the box is carried
Upon the restless foam:
It goes a thousand miles or more,
Till washed up on a desert shore.

And there the box is opened
By Big Chief Worrisome,
He takes your troubles one by one
And holds them up to catch the sun.

Some are to him as jewels,
And others, little gems,
But most of them he'll toss aside,
For worthless fakes he can't abide.

The Three Salesmen

A double glazing salesman chap
Came to my house and said:
'Half your heat goes through the doors
Or windows, I'm afraid.'

A cavity foam insulation chap
Then came and butted in:
'Half your heat goes through the walls
And isn't kept within.'

An attic insulation chap
Then argued in reply:
'Half your heat goes through the roof.'
At that point, so did I.

Whatnot

There's a shop in the High Street that deals in antiques,
And I've looked in the window for weeks and for weeks,
But I've not yet been able to understand why
The price of a Whatnot should be quite so high.

A Thingumabob wouldn't be such a price,
A What-you-may-call-it would *look* just as nice,
But neither of these things would cost half as much,
And you buy them in shops where you're welcome to touch.

An Oojamaflip is as rare and as big,
And so for that matter's a Thingumajig,
But neither of these is expensive to buy,
So why is the price of a Whatnot so high?

39

Let Basil go to Basildon

Let Basil go to Basildon,
Let Lester go to Leicester;
Let Steven go to Stevenage
With raincoat and sou'wester.

Let Peter go to Peterhead,
Let Dudley go to Dudley;
Let Milton go to Milton Keynes –
The pavements there are puddly.

Let Felix go to Felixstowe,
Let Barry go to Barry;
Let Mabel go to Mablethorpe,
But I at home shall tarry.

Let Alice go to Alice Springs,
Let Florence go to Florence;
Let Benny go to Benidorm
Where rain comes down in torrents.

Let Winnie go to Winnipeg,
Let Sidney go to Sydney;
Let Otto go to Ottawa –
I am not of that kidney.

Let Vera go to Veracruz,
Let Nancy go to Nancy,
But I'll stay home while others roam –
Abroad I do not fancy.

My Uncle's Umbrella

Under my uncle's umbrella
Are Uncle Augustus and I.
My uncle's quite fat –
If it wasn't for that,
I'd manage to keep myself dry.

Rolling down a Hill

I'm rolling
rolling
rolling
down

I'm rolling
down a
hill.

I'm rolling
rolling
rolling
down

I'm rolling
down it
still.

I'm rolling
rolling
rolling
down

I'm rolling
down a
hill

I'm rolling
rolling
rolling
down

But now
I'm feeling
ill.

Sir Percy's Problem

There lived a knight long years ago
Who wasn't very nice to know.
When other knights soaked in a bath
In wooden tub before the hearth,
Sir Percival just shook his head
And took a book and went to bed.
Oh, how he hated suds and soap,
The mere thought made him moan and mope.

Thus never did he wash his feet;
His hair was never brushed and neat;
He never sank into a tub
To give his back a good old scrub;
Nor did he wash behind his ears,
(And this went on for years and years!)
And with a bath so overdue,
No wonder that his friends were few.

The dragons that he sought to slay
Surrendered when he came their way,
He left them writhing on their backs –
No need to use his battleaxe –
And damsels who were in distress
Soon overcame their helplessness
And told him things were now all right
And that they didn't need a knight.

At last the day came when he went
Into a strange establishment –
A building that was dark and dim,
Quite unfamiliar to him;
But keen Sir Percival had heard
That awful things therein occurred:
Deeds far too dark to mention here,
They'd fill you full of dread and fear.

Suffice to say, Sir Percival
Was not afraid of that at all;
So in he went, to face the foe,
The likes of which he didn't know.
But entering the hallway grim,
A sudden change came over him.
He started shaking as with fright.
And soon became a nervous knight.

What did he see to make him shake?
What made him in his armour quake?
What gave him such a foul surprise?
The fearsome sight that filled his eyes
Was seven maidens armed with mops
And buckets brimming to their tops
With disinfectant which they sloshed
All over him till he was washed.

And when they'd cleaned him then they went
And soaked him in a vat of scent
Which he emerged from smelling sweet
As roses, from his head to feet.
But how Sir Percy hated it,
He didn't like the smell a bit:
It took the best part of a year
For it to wholly disappear.

But when he was restored at last
To the old Percy of the past,
He slunk away to find a place
Far from the wretched human race.
It's thought he found a distant cave
Where he could still be bold and brave
And where he lived for all his time
With warthogs in the dirt and grime.

Barge Pole

Poetry?
I wouldn't touch it with a barge pole.

Well,
How about:
A long pole,
A lean pole,
A bamboo or
A bean pole?
A flag pole,
A tent pole,
A barber's or
A bent pole?
A green pole,
A grey pole,
A curtain or
A may pole?
A whole pole,
A half pole,
A great big
Telegraph pole?

No!
Not any sort –
No small pole,
No large pole –
I wouldn't touch it with a barge pole.

Juggler Jim

I'm Jim and I juggle
A jug and a jar
And junkets and jelly
And jam.
With jovial, joyful
And jocular jests,
How jolly a jester
I am!

Borderline Case

'You're a borderline case,'
They said to my face.
'A borderline case?'
I sighed in disgrace.
'Yes, borderline case –
Get out of this place.'

So I went to the border,
Still not knowing
If I were coming
Or if I were going.
And I found the border
And stood on the line,
But nobody wanted
A case like mine.

For 'No,' said the left camp,
And 'No,' said the right.
(For a borderline case is
An unwelcome sight.)
But along the border
Then I could see
Some other sorts
Who looked like me.

So I went to them,
And the smile on their faces
Told me that here was
The best of all places,
Amongst all the other
Borderline cases.

The Trough

I wonder if my pony knows
When he's drinking from his trough
It's really our old bathtub with
The enamel all worn off?

I wonder, *is* he unaware,
Or does he pause and think:
'Long years ago, here bathed Aunt Maud,'
Before he takes a drink?

The Echo

I passed a cave,
I stopped outside,
And in I walked,
'Hello!' I cried.
'Hello' my echoed
Voice replied,
'Hello hello hello.'

I stood awhile
Then turned about
And sighed, 'Goodbye,'
As I came out.
'Goodbye!' I heard
My echo shout,
'Goodbye goodbye goodbye!'

Have You Ever?

Have
you
ever
perched
a
poem
on
your
nose?

Have you
ever worn
a verse
upon your
clothes?

Have you ever sniffed a sonnet in a rose?

Have you caught   rhyme   it
ever   a   before   goes?

Establishment

Let's all go to the establishment!
Let's all go to what establishment?
Let's all go to the establishment with automatic washing
machines!
*Let's all go to the establishment with automatic washing machines
for whose use?*
Let's all go to the establishment with automatic washing
machines for public use!
No thanks, I must go to the launderette . . .

Uncle Paul

My Uncle Paul makes lots and lots
Of extra–ordinary pots.
I only wish one day he'd choose
To make a pot that we could *use*.

Archibald's Progress

Archibald liked pulling faces,
All day long he'd make grimaces,
And at school he'd taunt his teachers
With contortions of his features.

Sitting at his school desk smugly,
Once he pulled a face so ugly,
That he gave poor Miss McKenzie
Cause to fly into a frenzy:

Mouth wide open – how revolting!
Tongue protruding – how insulting!
Puffed-out cheeks and wrinkled forehead –
Archibald looked really horrid!

Thus it was the nasty creature
So provoked his gentle teacher,
That she, driven to distraction,
Took at once most drastic action.

Pelting him with books, she dented
Archie's head till he repented,
And agreed that when at places
Such as school, he'd not pull faces.

Let us now praise Miss McKenzie,
She who flew into a frenzy,
And in just one scripture session,
Made a permanent impression.

Ben

Ben's done something really bad,
He's forged a letter from his dad.
He's scrawled:

Dear Miss,
            Please let Ben be
Excused this week from all P.E.
He's got a bad cold in his chest
And so I think it might be best
If he throughout this week could be
Excused from doing all P.E.

I hope my ~~wright~~ writing's
            not too bad.

      Yours sincerely,
      (signed) Ben's Dad.

Winter Term

Headmasters and headmistresses
Have chopped the year in three:
We've autumn, spring and summer terms,
But where can winter be?

What have they done with winter? Do
They think they're being kind
In making us feel winter is
A figment of the mind?

It seems that winter's been condensed
To just two weeks or three,
Renamed the Christmas holiday –
That's how it seems to me.

Gordon Glass

Every single time Miss Muffin
Puts a question to our class,
Who is always first to answer?
Need I ask? It's Gordon Glass.

He can tell you quite precisely
What's the boiling point of glue,
The capital of Venezuela,
The population of Peru.

And he knows his nine times table,
He knows the square root of π.
He can add, divide, subtract or
Gordon Glass can multiply.

He knows all about the Ice Age
Or the War of Jenkins' Ear,
Pitt the Younger, Pitt the Elder,
Bonaparte and Boadicea.

Gordon Glass has all the answers,
But one thing still bothers me:
Most our class are aged eleven,
Gordon Glass is thirty-three.

Plodders

We homeward plod, our satchels full
Of books to make our evenings dull.
We homeward plod, our heads hung low,
Crammed full of facts One Ought to Know.

Tomorrow we will plod once more
To school, where we will stay till four,
Or thereabouts, for that is when,
With books, we'll homeward plod again.

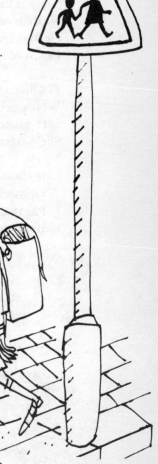

A Blackpool Ballad

At *Two Fat Ladies* Tower View
Lived lonely lovelorn Dick,
Who loved a girl along the way
At number *Clickety Click*.

Sue was the lass from Lancashire
He'd loved since he was seven:
He loved her hair, he loved her eyes,
He loved her *Legs Eleven*.

But Sue, she loved a lad called Jim,
Who worked the Bingo Hall;
Each night till half past *Maggie's Den*
She'd listen to him call.

One night, when Dick saw them embrace,
With rage he shook his fist,
For Susan, who was *Sweet Sixteen*,
He thought had ne'er been kissed.

Cried Dick to Jim, 'Let go of her!
Sweet Sue, I love thee more.
Please take, now I am come of age,
My own *Key of the Door*.'

Jim laughed aloud at such a vow
And sneered, 'I'm sorry, mate,
But I'm the *Kelly's Eye* for Sue –
We've fixed upon a date!'

As poor heart-broken Dick sloped off
Across the prom from Jim,
A Number Thirteen tram appeared –
Unlucky 'twas for him.

*   *   *

They buried Dick beneath the sands,
And as the mourners passed,
Sighed Sue, 'Love's like a Bingo Game,
His number's up at last.'

Trampoline

I'm sorry to disturb you, miss, I hate to intervene,

But could you for a moment, please, put down your magazine?

I've got a hundred pounds to spend, and I am really keen,

If you could only serve me, miss, to buy this trampoline.

£99.99

PLEASE PAY HERE

Certificates

Certificates, certificates,
That's what I've got a lot of:

My first one, tatty and torn,
Shows that I was born.
My next shows I can tie my laces,
And the ones after that
Tell you I'm pretty good at
Riding my bicycle round obstacles
And at winning three-legged
And egg-and-spoon races.

Yes, certificates, certificates,
That's what I've got a lot of.

I've got one for coming second in
A Road Safety Poster Design Competition
For the under seventeens,
And one for passing 'O' level Maths,
And one for doing a length and a half
At the local swimming baths
At Milton Keynes.

Yes, certificates, certificates,
That's what I've got a lot of.

I don't get many nowadays,
But I'll get one if I wed
And I'm sure to get another
Which I'll pick up when I'm dead.

Yes, certificates, certificates,
That's what I'll have a lot of.

Four Tongue Twisters

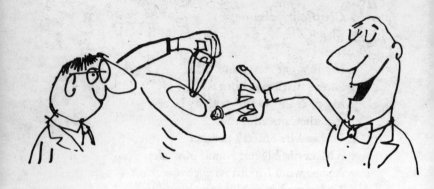

Here's a cymbal for the singer
With a thimble on his finger:
See the singer with a thimble
On his finger thump the cymbal!

I used to think my whites were white
Until I saw the whiter whites
Of Mrs White whose whiter whites
Were whiter than my whites were.

It's just a myth
That Mrs Smith's mother
Misses Mrs Moss.
She misses Mrs Moss
No more than Mrs Moss's mother
Misses Mrs Smith.

Hooray,
Hoorah!
Here's
A
Gay
Hussar.
Hoorah,
Hooray!
A
Hussar
Who's
Gay!

The Missing Eskimo

There is an igloo far away
Without an Eskimo;
Now, could a blizzard yesterday
Have buried him in snow?

Or did he in his kayak go
Till he could go no more,
And so today our Eskimo
Sits on some foreign shore?

I saw a polar bear last night
Who looked a hungry beast;
Perhaps he gave our friend a fright
And made of him a feast?

Or did he, on some distant floe
Walk where the ice was thin,
And thus our hapless Eskimo
Fell through and tumbled in?

Or on the other hand, perhaps,
He went off on his sledge,
But having crossed the Land of Lapps
Was dragged clean off the edge?

The possibilities, I'd say
Are endless. All I know
Is, there's an igloo far away
Without an Eskimo . . .

Yo-yo

Yes, you may use my yo-yo
My yo-yo made of yew.
My yellow yo-yo made of yew
Is yours to use in Yeovil,
And York and Yarmouth too.
Yea, use my yo-yo yonder
Till it gets used to you,
And yodel as you use it,
My yo-yo made of yew.

Joe

We don't mention Joe
In this house any more;
No, not since he nailed
Mother's boots to the floor.
What makes matters worse
With regard to this crime
Is Mother was wearing
Her boots at the time.

Wobble-dee-woo

What would you do
With a Wobble-dee-woo?
Would you eat it
Or wear it
Or play it?
What would you do
With a Wobble-dee-woo?
(I've only just learned
How to say it.)

What would you do
With a Wobble-dee-woo?
Would you wear it
Or play it
Or eat it?
What would you do
With a Wobble-dee-woo?
(I'm sorry, I'll have
To repeat it.)

What would you do
With a Wobble-dee-woo?
Would you play it
Or eat it
Or wear it?
What would you do
With a Wobble-dee-woo?
(It's driving me mad,
I can't bear it!)

74

School Day

Break-time, break-time,
Hurry up, hurry up.

Lunch-time, lunch-time,
Hurry up, hurry up.

Break-time, break-time,
Hurry up, hurry up.

Home-time, home-time,
Hurry up, hurry up.

Commuter

Oh, I'm a glad commuter
And I'm travelling by train.
I work with a computer
With a really clever brain.

Now I'm a sad commuter
As the train transports me back:
My clever old computer
Has just given me the sack.

Me

There's a film that everybody's seen
But me.
There's a place that everybody's been
But me.
There's a tape that everybody's got
But me.
But there's something everybody's *not*
– That's Me!

The Cat and the King

A cat may look at a king
And a king may look at a cat.
If thin the cat and fat the king,
There isn't much danger in *that*,
But just suppose fat is the cat,
Conversely, thin the king,
The king gets mighty cross at that,
And stamps like anything.

Frank's Chair

I remember the barber we went to
As boys, where Old Frank cut our hair,
I remember the hard bench we sat on
Whilst waiting to sit in His Chair.

I remember the curls all around us –
The silver, the dark and the fair –
I remember Old Frank in his long coat
As we went up to sit in His Chair.

I remember the shelves full of bottles,
And the smock that we all had to wear.
I remember the snipping and clipping
From Frank as we sat in His Chair.

I remember the itchy-neck feeling
And the stuff that he sprayed on our hair.
I remember the half-crown we paid him
For braving Old Frank and His Chair.

Pogo Stick

Upon my pogo stick I pounce
And out of school I homeward bounce.
I bounce so high, how my heart pounds
Until at last I'm out of bounds.

Mr Burton

Mr Burton drives a bus:
He frequently delivers us
From the depot to the station,
Or some other destination,
Such as school or shopping centre.
(You just pay him as you enter.)

But on Sundays, Mr Burton
Hasn't got his busman's shirt on,
Or his busman's tie or hat on,
No, he's nothing quite like *that* on,
For on that day in his bungal-
Ow, he's Tarzan of the Jungle.

80

Something made of three wash leathers
Is his wardrobe in all weathers.
Meanwhile Betty (Mrs Burton),
Puts a sort of furry skirt on,
After which, she and her spouse
Stamp and hollo through the house.

All day long, behind closed curtains,
Thus amuse themselves the Burtons,
Jane and Tarzan every Sunday,
But at 8 a.m. on Monday,
He clocks in at the terminus,
And Mr Burton drives a bus.

Moggy

The moggy needs his mistress
To bring him milk and meat,
But when I hear the mistress
Calling in the street
For her mog who's missing,
Who's been an hour lost,
I wonder, mog or mistress,
Who needs the other most?

My Dog

My dog is well-equipped to hear
A note too high for human ear:
With ears so big they reach the ground,
No wonder he hears every sound.

Sabre-toothed Tigers

It's pointless being polite
If sabre-toothed tigers attack;
So if they're beginning to bite,
Be bold for a bit and bite back.

The Wildebeest

The Wildebeest bewilders me,
His horns are frightful as can be,
A fiercer sight I've yet to see,
With hair so thick and black.
He'll kick and buck and leap and rear
If you should ever venture near,
But though he'll fill you full of fear,
He never will attack.

The Wildebeest bewilders me,
He's from a funny family,
Half-horse, half-ox he seems to be
Who's much inclined to mope.
And yet this grotesque creature who
Is commonly known as the gnu,
Is merely, in the experts' view,
A humble antelope.

Octopus

Last Saturday I came across
Most nonchalant an octopus;
I couldn't help but make a fuss,
And shook him by the tentacle.

He seemed to find it all a bore
And asked me, 'Have we met before?
I'm sorry, but I can't be sure,
You chaps all look identical.'

Lost Gloves

Impaled upon the railings
Are the lost gloves –
Leather fingers point skyward in despair;
Woollen ones, dejected, hang forlorn.
And each neglected, useless mitten
Seems to warn those passing by:
'Beware!'

Pullover

To pull the wool over
To pull the wool over
To pull the wool over
Your eyes,
Try on a pullover
Try on a pullover
Try on a pullover
For size.

Dressing Gown

Why do people
I'm addressing
Frown
When I've got on
My dressing
Gown?
And some give me
A dressing
Down
When I've got on
My dressing
Gown?

I'll be in the Wardrobe, Wilma

I'll be in the wardrobe, Wilma,
If you should ever call,
Or putting up a chandelier,
Or papering a wall.

And I'll be too tired to answer,
If you should ever phone,
And, Wilma, though it grieves me so,
I need to be alone.

I'll be up the chimney, Wilma,
If you should ever write,
Too busy to reply to you,
I'm up there day and night.

But if you *should* bump into me
One day when I'm off-guard,
I'll say, 'You must drop in some time,
Sweet Wilma, here's my card!'

Peter

I'm not sitting next to Peter
For he's such a messy eater,
And although he's my own brother,
Can't we swap him for another?
(For I'd so prefer a sibling
Who is not forever dribbling.)

Maybe to an Elephant

Maybe to an elephant
You're pretty.
Maybe to an elephant
You're cute.
Maybe to an elephant
You're elegant
And eloquent
And ever so intelligent
To boot.
But this is all irrelevant –
The claims of any elephant
I strongly would
Refute!

The Ventriloquists' Convention

The Ventriloquists' Convention
Will be gathering tonight:
Rhymes too humorous to mention
To themselves they will recite.

All the audience are dummies.
(It's the only sort they've got.)
They have wooden heads and tummies,
But they laugh an awful lot.

Rosemary's Friends

O, Rosemary's friends are her mantelshelf folk:
A shepherd, two sweethearts, a milkmaid with yoke,
And grandest of all is a cricketer chap
Who stands at the wicket in flannels and cap,
Awaiting a ball that's about to be bowled,
For years he's been batting – no wonder he's old;
But happy is Rosie to have such a man
And yesterday morning she told me her plan:
'I'm off to have tea with W. G. Grace
And polish the porcelain beard on his face.'

Yesterday, Today and Tomorrow

Yesterday I threw away
The day.
There seemed so little to be done,
And the day, it just went on and on.

Today is different,
Today
There seem so many things to do,
And the day is only halfway through.

Tomorrow, I wonder,
I wonder,
Will I throw the thing away,
Or live each moment of the day?

Our Coconut Mat

We have a mat
Of coconut
At our front door
With WELCOME on it.

And everyone
Who enters our house
Is welcomed in
By our coconut mat.

But when somebody
  comes
I'd rather not see,
I turn around
Our coconut mat.

So when they leave,
To face the rain,
They're welcomed *out*
By our coconut mat.

Dining with Duke Humphrey

Duke Humphrey's coming to dine tonight,
Let's light the chandelier.
Duke Humphrey's coming to dine tonight,
Let's raise a glass of cheer.
Duke Humphrey's coming to dine tonight,
The time is drawing near;
Duke Humphrey's coming to dine tonight,
You'd hardly know he's here . . .

Poems, Poems Everywhere

Poems, poems everywhere,
In my ears and in my hair,
In my shoes and in my socks,
In my desk and pencil box,
In my bath and in my bed,
In my heart and in my head.
Please read my books when you have time
And rid me of my life of rhyme.